Letter from the Author to Jane.

Our given names are just that: names that are given to us when we are newborns or very little children. Sometimes we change them when we grow up but more often than not, the name we are given by our parents is generally the one we live with all our lives. We just have to hope that it is one that inspires us to be the best person we possibly can be and an aid to our treating others with kindness and a gentle heart.

I hope you are happy with your name and its meaning. The short definition given on this cover is meant to gladden you, but if not, let it be a springboard to digging deeper into your name's meaning. Often when you pinpoint the exact time in history its use started or why, you will find that you can better understand its definition. This is what happened with my own name, Melanie. :)

I find onomastics or onomatology—the study of names—extremely interesting, and always have, hence the reason for this "What Your Name Means" series of notebooks (by the way, onoma is the Greek word for "name"—easy to understand now, right?)

Please join my MAILING LIST to learn about new "What Your Name Means" notebooks and, if you would like to request a specific name for a notebook, please email me and let me know.
I hope you have happy times with your notebook, Jane!

Sincerely,
Melanie Ann
melanieannauthor@gmail.com

To:

- *join my mailing list,*
- *request a specific name for a notebook or*
- *to get a list of published, WHAT YOUR NAME MEANS Notebooks, and their direct Amazon link,*

please contact me here:

melanieannauthor@gmail.com

Made in the USA
Monee, IL
24 December 2021

87094043R00031